Riches of the Earth

Rice

Irene Franck and David Brownstone

GROLIER

An imprint of Scholastic Library Publishing
Danbury, Connecticut

Credits and Acknowledgments

abbreviations: t (top), b (bottom), l (left), r (right), c (center)

Image credits: Agricultural Research Service Library: 1b (detail), 7r, and 11 (Keith Weller), 12 (Scott Bauer), 22 (David Nance); Art Resource: 15 (Scala), 16 (Manu Sassoonian), 20 (Newark Museum, Gift of Christine Bates and Peter W. Greenough); Getty Images/PhotoDisc: 3 and 5 (C Squared Studios), 10l (John A. Rizzo); Getty Images/PhotoDisc/PhotoLink: 4 (S. Meltzer), 6 (M. Freeman), 13, 18-19l (D. Falconer), 29; National Aeronautics and Space Administration (NASA): 1t and running heads; Photo Researchers, Inc.: 7l (Scott Camazine), 10r (TH Foto/Tschanz-Hofmann/OKAPIA), 23 (Blair Seitz), 24l (Fred McConnoughey), 27 (Jim Steinberg); U.S. Department of Agriculture: 25t, 25b; Woodfin Camp & Associates: 8-9l (Leo Touchei), 19r (David Austen), 24r (Kal Muller), 28 (Michael Yamashita); World Bank: 17 (Edwin Huffman), 22 and 26 (Ray Witlin). Original images drawn for this book by K & P Publishing Services: 9r, 14.

Our thanks to Joe Hollander, Phil Friedman, and Laurie McCurley at Scholastic Library Publishing; to photo researchers Susan Hormuth, Robin Sand, and Robert Melcak; to copy editor Michael Burke; and to the librarians throughout the northeastern library network, in particular to the staff of the Chappaqua Library—director Mark Hasskarl; the expert reference staff, including Martha Alcott, Michele J. Capozzella, Maryanne Eaton, Catherine Paulsen, Jane Peyraud, Paula Peyraud, and Carolyn Reznick; and the circulation staff, headed by Barbara Le Sauvage—for fulfilling our wide-ranging research needs.

Published 2003 by Grolier
Division of Scholastic Library Publishing
Old Sherman Turnpike
Danbury, Connecticut 06816

For information address the publisher:
Scholastic Library Publishing, Grolier Division
Old Sherman Turnpike, Danbury, Connecticut 06816

Library of Congress Cataloging-in-Publication Data

Franck, Irene M.
    Rice / Irene Franck and David Brownstone.
      p. cm. -- (Riches of the earth ; v. 9)
    Summary: Provides information about rice and its importance in everyday life.
    Includes bibliographical references and index.
    ISBN 0-7172-5730-4 (set : alk. paper) -- ISBN 0-7172-5721-5 (vol. 9 : alk paper)
    1. Rice--Juvenile literature [1. Rice.] I. Brownstone, David M. II. Title.

SB191.R5F72 2003
633.1'8--dc21
2003044085

Printed in the United States of America

Designed by K & P Publishing Services

Contents

Rice: Food for Billions

Polished white rice like this is favored by billions of people around the world, though it is not as nutritious as brown rice.

Most of us think of rice as just one of the many foods we eat. We know and often like it as a standard kind of food found in Chinese, Japanese, Indian, and other Asian cooking. Some of us like it even more when we eat it in such breakfast cereals as rice flakes, shredded rice, and puffed rice. We also find rice in baby foods, rice cakes, and cookies. We use rice in cooking, in the form of cooking oils, baking powders, and rice vinegars. Some people also drink rice products, such as the very popular Japanese rice wine

sake and several more Chinese and other Asian rice wines. Possibly most of all, we think of rice as we do potatoes and noodles—as the kind of basic food that goes along with such "main" dishes as meat, poultry, and fish.

For a large part of the world's people, however, rice is far more than just one of many foods. For them it is the most important food of all, the basic source of the nourishment they need to live.

However, as grown and as normally prepared, rice is not as complete and healthy a food as some other cereal grains, such as wheat. That is especially so when some nutritious parts of the rice have been removed during processing (see p. 26).

Until the 1960s there was not enough rice to feed Asia's fast-growing populations, and famine was in sight in many countries. However, then the quality and quantity of the world's rice and several other cereal grains began to improve a great deal.

Plant scientists were able to develop new, higher-yielding varieties of rice that were also far more resistant to disease and pests than earlier varieties. Scientists were also able to develop varieties that could grow faster than earlier varieties. This made it possible to produce two or even three rice crops per year, when earlier only one per year had been possible.

Today rice is the main food of at least one billion people, most of them from some of the world's

For many people around the world, rice is their main food of the day. If they are lucky, they will have other foods to go with it, like these tasty-looking shrimp.

poorest countries. For hundreds of millions of others, rice is a major diet element. Even the slightest improvement in the world's rice supply has been tremendously helpful in fighting against mass hunger and disease.

This development of healthier, higher-yielding crops was called the *Green Revolution*. Later some problems arose. The new crops cost more to produce, needing expensive chemicals that poor farmers often could not afford. Some chemicals also poisoned the environment (see p. 21), seeming to cause more harm than good. Despite continuing problems, many poor people have had more and healthier rice to eat because of such improvements.

In the late 1900s scientists also began to make changes in the rice plant's genes, the basic biological codes that guide its growth and development. This *genetic engineering* has developed new and attractive varieties of rice. However, it has also raised concerns that altering a plant's genetic code might damage people and the environment. The long-term effects of such genetic changes are still unknown.

In poor areas of the world, every possible bit of land is turned into space for growing. Flat terraces like these are cut into steep hillsides, which otherwise would not be suitable for planting rice.

What Is Rice?

The outer covering of the rice kernel is green when young, as here. At the end of the growing season, it loses its color and turns beige or very light brown, like the rest of the plant.

This is one of the long-grain rices that are commonly grown in the United States.

The edible part of the rice plant—the part we eat—is the *kernel* (seed), a cereal grain that is a small piece of the rice plant. The rice plant is a member of the grass family, as are wheat, barley, oats, rye, and corn (maize). All together, these are the main food grains that have been feeding the world's peoples since the beginning of farming, at least 10,000 years ago.

Especially in Asia and the world's other main rice-growing regions, rice is also commonly called *paddy*, and a field in which rice is grown is often called a *rice paddy*. Rice seeds that have been harvested and had their outer cov-

This is what the harvested and dried rice grains look like before the outer coverings—the hull and the bran—are removed.

erings (*husks*) removed are seldom called *paddy*. However, rice still growing in a field, or harvested and as yet unhusked, is often called either *paddy* or *rice*.

The rice plant is a green grass. It usually ranges in size from four to six feet tall, but there are larger and smaller varieties. Some of the very small, or *dwarf*, varieties may be only a few inches high.

Each rice plant grows from a single seed. The body of the rice plant is made up of its roots, stem, leaves, and *panicle*, a cluster of flowers in the head of the plant. Within the panicle grow "spikelets," which become individual flowers. During rice's growing season, a grain of rice develops within each flower.

As the rice plant grows, it uses water and nutrients (nourishing substances) drawn in through its roots. Its green leaves also use sunlight, carbon dioxide (a common gas) from the air, and water to make various sugars, in a process called *photosynthesis*. These sugars are the rice plant's main source of energy.

The Rice Grain

Each rice grain has four main parts. The first is the hard *hull* of the grain, which surrounds and protects the seed. After harvesting, the hull must be removed before rice can be eaten.

The largest part of the rice grain—80 to 90 percent—is the *endosperm*, which is white. The endosperm is composed mainly of carbohydrates. These are chemical compounds (mixed materials) that supply most of rice's energy-giving food to humans. The carbohydrates in the endosperm amount to more than 60 percent of the whole kernel.

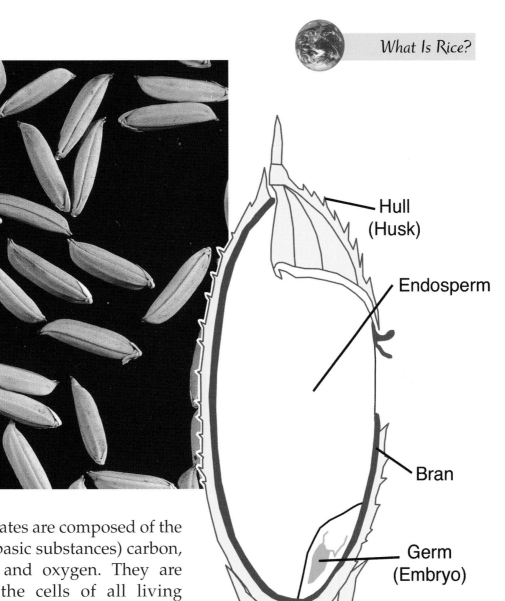

Carbohydrates are composed of the elements (basic substances) carbon, hydrogen, and oxygen. They are found in the cells of all living things and are necessary to life. The carbohydrates found in rice contain energy-supplying starch and several sugars, along with necessary fiber (*cellulose*).

Another key part of the rice grain is the *bran*. This thin brown layer under the hull contains much of rice's vitamins, minerals, and other health-giving substances.

If the bran layer is left on during processing, the result is called *brown rice*. If the bran layer is removed, the

This is a cutaway view of a single rice grain. The beige-colored hull covers the nutritious dark brown bran, an inner layer that is often removed. Inside the bran is the white endosperm, plus the small germ (embryo). When the hull, bran, and germ are removed, the result is the familiar white rice grain.

result is *white rice*. Brown rice is far healthier, because it keeps the valuable nutrients in its bran, while these are lost in white rice. This makes white rice much less nourishing than not only brown rice but also wheat and some other grains.

Unfortunately, most people around the world prefer polished white rice. It is thought to look and taste better. It is also easier to cook with other foods and easier for our bodies to digest (break apart to get the nutrients). Because of this, the bran is removed from most rice after harvesting. To somewhat make up for the loss of the bran, some rice processors add vitamins and other substances to their white rice products, then calling them *enriched* or *fortified*.

Inside the rice kernel is a very small part called the *germ* (or *embryo*). By the time the rice is har-

This is what brown rice looks like after the husk has been removed and before it is cooked. The brown covering is the bran, which is very nutritious. If that is removed, the result is the familiar white rice, which is tasty but less nutritious.

Dark brown rice turns light brown when cooked, as shown here served with fish and vegetables.

This rice grower (left) and research scientist are examining plants in a field of Akita Komachi rice. That is one of the many varieties of Japonica rice that are grown around the world.

vested, the germ has become a seed within a seed. When a whole grain of rice is planted, the new rice plant will grow from that tiny germ inside the planted seed.

Nutrients in rice also include proteins, fat, and small but necessary amounts of vitamins, minerals, and other substances. The amounts vary greatly. They depend on the variety of rice, the climate, the other growing conditions, and how it was processed after harvesting, especially whether it is brown rice or white rice.

Varieties of Rice

Plant scientists have so far identified at least 80,000 cultivated (deliberately grown) varieties of rice. However, a single main kind of edible rice (*Oryza sativa*, usually abbreviated *O. sativa*) is cultivated throughout the world today. (*Oryza* is the Latin word for *rice*.) There is also a second kind of edible rice (*O. glaberrima*), which is grown in West Africa, but it is little used elsewhere.

There are three kinds of *O. sativa*. The first kind (*Indica*) is grown in most of the hot tropical regions of Asia. The second (*Javanica*) is grown in the hot tropical regions of Indonesia. The third (*Japonica*) is grown in warm-to-temperate regions, as in Japan and some parts of China. Outside of Asia's tropical regions, most of the world's rice is some variety of *Japonica*.

Several kinds of qualities are found within these broad classes of rice. Different varieties have grains of different lengths and shapes. Those varieties that tend to have long, thin grains are called *long grain*. Those that have somewhat shorter but still mostly thin grains are called *medium grain*. Those that have the shortest and fattest grains are called *short grain*. There are tens of thousands of varieties within these general categories. The long-grain varieties, often called *Carolina rices*, are those most favored in international trade.

All three main categories of rice include varieties that are composed of *hard rice*, which tends not to stick together when cooking. These are the main kinds of rice varieties used throughout the world. However, all three categories also include varieties composed of grains that do tend to stick together when cooking. These are the *glutinous rices*, often favored in Japan and Korea. When cooked, they tend to taste and smell sweeter than the other varieties.

Scientists are constantly trying to improve rice, to make it a better food for more people. The rice at the bottom here is a "parent" variety. The other two heads of rice are improved versions of the parent.

Chili and rice is a classic dish in the Americas, as shown here with some cornbread. However, rice did not arrive in the Americas until the late 1400s, when Europeans brought it across the Atlantic.

Rice around the World

China is the world's leading rice-producing country by far, with India a strong second. Many other Asian countries are also major rice producers. Most rice is eaten where it is produced or nearby. This means that the main rice-producing countries are also the world's leading rice-consuming countries.

Rice is also produced in a great many other countries. Its many varieties will grow well in a wide range of temperatures and soils—as long as the rice has enough water. Water, climate, soil, and several other key factors in rice-growing come together in near-tropical and warm Asian countries. Rice flourishes best of all in warm-to-hot southern, southeastern, and eastern Asia. An estimated 90 percent of the world's rice is grown there.

Among the world's most productive rice-growing countries are China, India, Pakistan, Myanmar (Burma), Malaysia, Thailand, Japan,

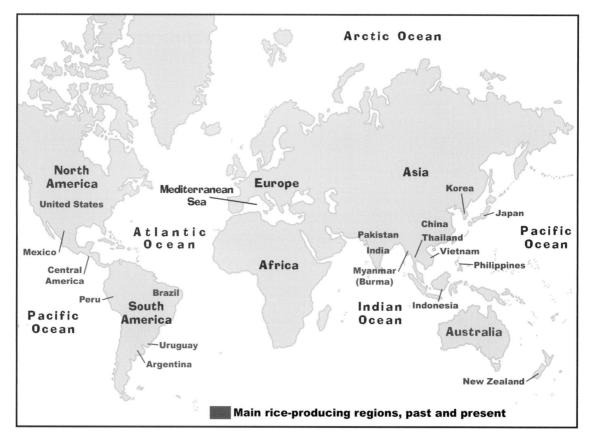

Main rice-producing regions, past and present

North Korea, South Korea, the Philippines, and Indonesia, all in Asia. Beyond that, some varieties of rice grow well in a wide band of countries that stretch right around the world, from the Americas to China and Indonesia. Rice's growing range has moved farther north and farther south during the late 20th century. New varieties and growing methods have made it possible to grow rice in cooler climates.

The United States is not one of the world's leading rice producers. However, unlike the major rice producers, the United States produces far more rice than it consumes.

Therefore it is one of the world's leading rice exporters to other countries. The main kinds of rice grown and exported are long-grain and medium-grain varieties. Most United States rice is grown on irrigated land, largely in southern California, southern Texas, Louisiana, and several other southern states.

Substantial amounts of rice are also grown in Mexico, Uruguay, Argentina, Peru, and Brazil. Much of the rice grown in other Central and South American countries is exported to Brazil, where more rice is eaten than grown.

For thousands of years many people have relied on rice as their main food, so the rice harvest is of major importance. Here a Japanese emperor (sheltered in the tent in the background) has come to view the rice crop being harvested in 1868.

Rice in History

Rice is one of the oldest cereal grains eaten by humans. People in what are now northern India and eastern Pakistan may have been gathering and eating rice growing wild 7,000 to 8,000 years ago (between 6000 B.C. and 5000 B.C.). That is probable, though not yet certain.

Chinese archaeologists have found evidence of rice farming (not just gathering of wild rice) in southern China dating back to 7,000 years ago. Widespread evidence indicates that by 6,000 years ago, rice was being farmed in a large region of East Asia, including what are now parts of northern India, southern China, Thailand, Myanmar (Burma), and Vietnam.

Rice cultivation spread after that, as new varieties were introduced that could grow well in a wide range of weather and water supply conditions. By 4,000 years ago rice farming was established in Japan, the Philippines, Indonesia, and throughout India and Pakistan.

By 2,000 to 2,500 years ago writings by Chinese historians make it clear that rice farming had spread throughout much of China. In the same period rice was moving westward across Asia into Persia (now Iran), Greece, Rome, and the other countries of southwest Asia and the Mediterranean world.

Rice farming continued to move west in the centuries that followed. Arab traders and soldiers returning from southwest Asia brought rice to northern Africa 1,500 years ago. After the European invasion of Asia began in the late 1400s, Europeans from many nations brought rice back home with them.

Like wheat and several other cereal grains, rice was not known in the Americas until it came across the Atlantic with European explorers, soldiers, and traders after the late 1400s. The Spanish, who conquered most of Central America and South America, brought rice with them. The Portuguese brought rice with them when they conquered Brazil. The British brought rice to Virginia and other southern East Coast colonies, starting in the 1640s.

Today substantial quantities of rice are also grown in Australia and New Zealand. Rice was introduced to both countries after they had become British colonies.

Rice farming came to the Americas only after Europeans arrived in the late 1400s. This painting by J. H. Wilner shows rice being harvested in Haiti, an island in the Caribbean.

Much of the work of growing rice is still done by hand in many parts of the world. Here in the Philippines, with the help of water buffaloes, workers are plowing the fields, getting them ready for planting rice seedlings. Sections to the lower left and beyond them have already been planted.

Planting and Growing Rice

Most rice grown in the world today is planted, grown, and harvested as it has been done for thousands of years. Modern machines and improved methods of farming could do the job faster and cheaper. However, most of the world's rice farmers are very poor people scratching out small livings on tiny plots of land, with the same kinds of inexpensive tools that have been in use for longer than anyone can remember. These long, old patterns are called *subsistence farming*, meaning that they produce just barely enough food to support the farmers.

These are rice seedlings, which have been carefully grown in a nursery. Now they are ready to be planted in a rice paddy.

These patterns are changing in our time, though often far too slowly. Crop yields—the amount of rice produced on a given piece of land—have improved tremendously in some areas. This is the result of reliable sources of water, improved farming methods, and higher-yielding varieties of rice that can better resist pests and disease. As these improvements spread, crop yields can certainly continue to rise.

Rice Cultivation

There are two basic ways of cultivating rice: in water or on dry land. The great majority of the world's rice is grown underwater. That is because crop yields are far higher grown in water than grown on dry land.

In water farming the rice plants are covered with water during their planting and cultivation in the field. At the end of the growing season the field is drained and the rice is harvested. The water may come from natural flooding of the field, as happens in some wet climates. It can also be supplied by irrigation—that is, bringing water from an outside source into fields through pipes or ditches.

In some areas large amounts of

Standing barefoot in a flooded field, this woman is planting rice seedlings, one by one. In much of the world, as here in Indonesia, this job continues to be done by hand.

water, as from heavy rains during a rainy season, are used to flood fields. In those situations rice plant stalks are said to "float." The plants very quickly grow as much as 20 feet high, as the tips of the plants seek the light they need to stay alive.

Growing rice on dry land means seeding, cultivating, and harvesting much as is done with other cereal grains, such as wheat.

Rice plants can be grown either directly from seeds planted in the ground or from *seedlings*. These are small rice plants grown from seeds in a *nursery* (a protected place for growing, such as a greenhouse or a sheltered field). These are then *transplanted*—moved and replanted— into the main rice fields.

Whether planted as seeds or as seedlings, rice plants can be planted wet or dry. When planted as seeds, they can be planted in several dif-

Even when rice fields are planted near rivers or streams, various devices are often needed to bring water into the fields themselves. This painting, *Working in the Rice Fields*, by 19th-century Korean artist Hyo Chong Yoo, shows a worker on a foot-operated water irrigation wheel.

ferent ways. These range from simple scattering into plowed furrows by hand all the way to planting by modern *seed drills*. The drills are machines that do the whole planting process in a single operation: cutting furrows (narrow trenches), measuring and depositing seeds, and then covering the furrows with earth.

During the rice plant's growing season, farmers must weed out other unwanted plants to help the rice plants get all the nourishment possible from the soil in the fields. Many times during the growing season, they must also turn over the earth between the furrows, to loosen and let air into (aerate) the earth. This helps the rice plants to grow. Farmers also try to find and destroy unwanted insects and other pests that can attack the growing rice plants.

Farmers may do these cultivating jobs using hand tools, such as basic hoes and harrows, to break up the ground. They may also use large, complicated machines. One such modern machine is the *cultivator*. It does several operations at once, including weed removal and turning over the earth.

Rice and Pesticides

Rice is not the only food grown in rice fields. Many flooded rice fields grow fish as a second crop. These provide valuable nutrients to a great many farm families. However, modern farming methods have created a serious problem: Chemicals called *pesticides* are used to kill damaging weeds, insects, and other pests. The problem is that they often also kill the fish in the flooded rice fields.

Pesticides are widely used throughout the world, and many have proven very useful. Yet at the same time some of them have proven terribly poisonous to plants, animals, people, and the environment.

In our time some particularly dangerous pesticides have been banned in the United States and many other countries. One of the most dangerous is the pesticide DDT (dichloro-diphenyl-trichloro-ethane), which was once the world's most widely used pesticide. It has been banned in the United States since 1972, though it and other banned chemicals are still used in many other countries, including some of the world's poorest.

This is one of the first varieties of rice to be developed by scientists in the Green Revolution. It is called a "semidwarf" rice because it does not grow very high. However, it grows more quickly and yields more grains than earlier varieties of rice.

In poorer areas around the world, much harvesting is still done by hand. These women are harvesting rice by hand from rice fields in Senegal.

Harvesting Rice

Most of the world's rice is grown in water, so the first step in harvesting is usually to drain rice-growing fields. For rice grown on dry land, no draining is necessary.

To prepare for harvesting, the farmer straightens out the heads of the rice plants growing in the fields. This allows them to be easily cut off during harvesting without damaging the grains.

The rice plants are then *reaped*— that is, workers cut off the grain-

carrying heads of the mature rice plants. Throughout eastern and southern Asia, reaping is most often done by hand. Farmers cut off the heads of rice plants one by one, with a short, sharp knife, a *sickle* (a short-handled knife with a curved blade), or a *scythe* (a larger version of a sickle). Such ancient hand tools have long been used for reaping rice and several other cereal grains. However, in many parts of the world, including the United States, machines are now more often used for reaping and other harvesting steps.

After reaping, the cut rice plant heads are stacked, usually in bundles called *sheaves*. To prevent spoilage, they must then be dried. Growing conditions, climate, and varieties of rice differ greatly, so there is no single recommended time set for drying. However, slow drying is generally preferred. If moisture is lost too quickly, the rice grains can be cracked and damaged.

Small power dryers have become the preferred tool for drying. That is because there is so much water left in rice fields even after draining, and because most rice is grown in very wet climates. However, many poor farmers cannot afford power dryers. To avoid spoilage of the reaped rice, many small farmers go directly on to the next step—*threshing*—after the rice has been reaped. However, some farmers without power dryers may dry their reaped rice in the sun for a short time first.

Threshing and Winnowing

Threshing is the process of separating rice grains from the rest of the rice plant. That can be done in any of several ways. Throughout Asia most threshing is done as it has been for thousands of years.

After harvesting, rice is often left to dry in the sun, as in this harvested rice field in the Philippines.

After the rice is threshed, it must be tossed in the air to separate the heavier grains from the lighter bits of husks and stems, a process called *winnowing*, as here in Indonesia.

After the harvesting and drying comes threshing, which separates the rice grains from the rest of the harvested rice plant. This Thai man is threshing some rice on a plastic sheet with a still-green rice field growing behind him.

One of the simplest, oldest—and most wasteful—ways to thresh rice is to spread the rice bundles on a hard floor and then trample them underfoot, drive farm animals over them, or run heavy wheeled machines over them. The aim is to smash the rice plants and so break the rice grains out of them. This is wasteful because many rice grains are also broken during the smashing. Modern threshing machines do the threshing job with far less waste. However, for most rice farmers, such machines are far too expensive.

However the threshing is done, the rice grains are separated from the rest of the plant. The result is a mass of rice grains, the rest of the broken-up rice plant, and whatever else was picked up in the fields and broken up in threshing.

The many and varied bits and pieces left are then separated out from the rice grains by *winnowing*. This process uses air flow to separate the heavier rice grains from the rest. Winnowing was traditionally done by workers tossing the rice matter by hand. Today many farmers instead use simple hand-operated or powered fans.

In some countries, as in the United States, threshing and winnowing are done largely by machine. Some such machines are called *combines* because they do all or almost all of the harvesting steps in a single operation: reaping, threshing, winnowing, and cleaning. These are like the combines that are now the main tools for harvesting most of the world's wheat.

Large harvesting machines are called *combines* because they literally combine many of the harvesting steps into a single pass. This combine is harvesting rice in the United States. The threshed rice is fed into the red wagon at the top left as the machine moves through the field.

This is a traditional mortar and pestle. It can be used to break up the rice hulls, so they can be removed. It can also be used, as here, to grind up rice and other grains. Two women from Burkina Faso, in Africa, are taking turns pounding with pestles.

Milling Rice

Milling is a group of processes aimed at removing the *hulls*, the hard outer covers of rice, also called *shells* or *husks*. Milling also includes cleaning the rice and removing the brown bran layers around the grain's white inside (its *endosperm*) and the grain's germ (see p. 9). The final result of the whole set of processes is creation of the kind of polished white rice favored by most people who eat rice.

When referring to rice, milling sometimes means only the grinding operation that removes the hard outer husk of the rice grains. The result is brown rice.

The basic processes of milling are the same whether it is done by hand in ancient ways or in a modern rice mill. Either way, the result is white rice—or brown rice—ready to cook and eat.

Most of the world's rice is still

milled in very simple old ways. This is because most rice farmers are very poor people, living and working in poor countries. Also most rice is eaten very close to home.

The simplest milling method is grinding with *mortar* and *pestle*. The grains are placed on a hard base (the *mortar*). Then they are smashed and broken by being pounded repeatedly with a heavy weight (the *pestle*). This process removes the hulls and most or all of the bran and germ. The pestle may be hand-driven or a modern machine using any kind of power source—the basic process is the same.

After most of the grain has been broken up by the pestle, it is cleaned, and the nongrain pieces are removed (*winnowed*). The process is then repeated until the rice is ready for cooking and eating.

Several improvements on this basic method are now used by some, but not many, rice farmers. Among those improvements are small power-driven machines that hull, clean, *pearl* (remove the bran layers), and polish the rice.

In many parts of the world, families share a threshing area and barn, as here on the Indonesian island of Bali. Rice is threshed on the ground, then put into sacks and stored in the barn until needed.

To feed people in the cities, rice grown in the rural areas is threshed, husked, put into bags, and shipped to large rice warehouses, like this one in Bangkok, Thailand.

them, under some pressure, through rollers made of rubber or harder substances. However, it does not wastefully pound them apart, as do the old mortar-and-pestle methods (see p. 26). The first pass through the rollers will remove most of the hulls. The rest are removed by repeated passes through the rollers.

After hulling, the rice kernels are brown, because they still have their coverings of bran. The kernels then move through rice milling machines. These remove the bran by any of several methods, depending on the design of the machine. Once the bran has been removed, the now-white rice is machine-polished, and the broken grains and leftover pieces are removed. The resulting shiny white rice is packaged for commercial use.

During the milling process several other substances and qualities may be added to rice. In several

Modern Rice Mills

Commercial rice mills use much more complicated machines to produce the kinds of more completely cleaned, hulled, pearled, and polished rice that is packaged and sold to consumers around the world.

At the start of the commercial milling process, unhulled rice is first thoroughly cleaned. Then it moves through a shelling machine. This removes the hulls by passing rice-producing countries, as in India, saffron and other spices are sometimes added during milling, for changed color, smell, and taste. Many other substances are also sometimes added to polish, shine, and whiten the milled rice even more.

Rice may also be *parboiled* before it is hulled. This process first places the unhulled rice grains in cold water and then hot water (or steam). This softens the rice inside the hull and makes it easier to hull the grain. Parboiling has long been popular in India.

Rice grains as harvested and milled are hard and dry, so they are easy to store and transport. When ready to be eaten, rice must be cooked (usually boiled or steamed) with water or some other liquid to soften it, so our bodies can digest (get nutrients from) it. Rice easily picks up flavors from spices or other foods, which is one reason it is so popular.

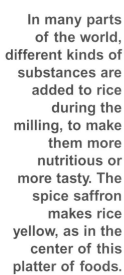

In many parts of the world, different kinds of substances are added to rice during the milling, to make them more nutritious or more tasty. The spice saffron makes rice yellow, as in the center of this platter of foods.

Words to Know

bran The brown outer edible cover of the rice KER-NEL, between the ENDOSPERM and the HULL.

brown rice Rice with its bran layer left on during processing. It is much more nourishing than *white rice*, which has had its bran removed.

carbohydrates Chemical compounds (mixed materials) found in living cells and necessary to human life. The carbohydrates in the rice kernel include STARCH, CELLULOSE, and several sugars.

cellulose A CARBOHYDRATE found in the ENDOSPERM of the rice KERNEL; also called *fiber*.

combine A farm machine that does all the rice harvesting processes in a single operation, including reaping (see REAPER), WINNOWING, and THRESHING.

edible Able to be eaten.

endosperm The main part of the KERNEL of a rice plant. After processing this becomes a grain of white rice (see BROWN RICE).

enriching Adding substances, such as vitamins and minerals, during the MILLING process to improve the quality of rice as a food.

fiber: See CELLULOSE.

furrow A long straight cut into a farm field in which crops are planted.

genetic engineering Making changes in *genes*, the basic set of biological codes that guide a plant's growth and development, to create better varieties.

germ The very small part of the rice KERNEL that is the seed from which a new rice plant can grow.

glutinous rice Rice varieties that tend to stick together when cooked.

grain: See KERNEL.

Green Revolution The development of new EDI-BLE plant varieties and farming methods, starting in the mid-20th century, that have greatly increased crop yields in many of the world's poorest countries.

hard rice Rice that does not tend to stick together during cooking.

harrow To break up and smooth over the earth in a field. Also the tool used to do this.

hull The hard outer covering of a rice KERNEL, which must be removed before rice can be eaten. Also called *husk* and *shell*.

husk: See HULL.

kernel The edible grain that is the seed of the rice plant.

long-grain rice Rice varieties with grains that

tend to be long and thin. *Medium-grain rice* is also thin but somewhat shorter, while *short-grain rice* tends to be shorter and fatter.

medium-grain rice: See LONG-GRAIN RICE.

milling A group of processes that includes cleaning rice and removing its HULL, BRAN, and GERM.

mortar and pestle A grinding method that removes rice HULLS by grinding KERNELS between a hard base (the *mortar*) and a hard, heavy weight (the *pestle*).

paddy Another name for *rice*. A field in which rice is grown is called a *rice paddy*.

panicle The cluster of flowers that grows within the head of the rice plant. Within a panicle grow flowers that will develop into rice KERNELS.

parboiling A method of softening the HULLS of unhulled rice KERNELS, by putting them into cold water and then into hot water or steam.

pesticides Chemicals used to kill weeds and insects that attack rice and other plants.

pestle: See MORTAR AND PESTLE.

photosynthesis A process by which the green leaves of plants make sugar from sunlight, carbon dioxide, and water.

proteins Basic chemical compounds (mixed substances) found in rice that are necessary to human life.

reaper A farming tool used to harvest growing plants. The term is used to describe a whole range of tools, from the early *sickle* and *scythe* to complicated, high-powered modern machines.

scythe: See REAPER.

seed drill A farming tool that cuts FURROWS, deposits measured amounts of seeds in them, and then covers the furrows.

shell: See HULL.

short-grain rice: See LONG-GRAIN RICE.

sickle: See REAPER.

sowing The process of seeding rice.

starch A kind of energy-supplying nutrient found in the CARBOHYDRATE part of the ENDOSPERM inside the KERNEL of a rice plant.

threshing Separating the rice KERNELS from the harvested rice plant.

white rice: See BROWN RICE.

winnowing Separating harvested rice from other parts of the broken-up rice plant, often by tossing them in the air.

On the Internet

The Internet has many interesting sites about rice. The site addresses often change, so the best way to find current addresses is to go to a search site, such as www.yahoo.com. Type in a word or phrase, such as "rice."

As this book was being written, websites about rice included:

http://www.riceweb.org/
RiceWeb, from the International Rice Research Institute (http://www.irri.org/), offering "facts and figures from the world of rice," including extensive information on history, growth, geography, production, research, a glossary, and more. The IRRI also offers the Rice Knowledge Bank: http://www.knowledgebank.irri.org/

http://www.asiarice.org/
Asia Rice Foundation website, offering information on rice's importance and cultural significance, plus research, recipes, photos, and links to other sites.

http://www.askasia.org/frclasrm/lessplan/l000008.htm
Part of the Asia Society website, offering lesson plans and educational activities about rice, including images of growth and production.

In Print

Your local library system will have various books on rice. The following is just a sampling of them.

Baker, H. G. *Plants and Civilization*. Belmont, CA: Wadsworth, 1978.
Fenton, Carroll Lane, and Herminie B. Kitchen. *The Plants We Live On*. New York: John Day, 1971.
Franck, Irene M., and David M. Brownstone. *The Green Encyclopedia*. New York: Prentice Hall, 1992.
Grist, D. H. *Rice*, 5th ed. London: Longman, 1985.
Heiser, Charles B. *Seed to Civilization*. San Francisco: W. H. Freeman, 1971.
Johnson, Sylvia A. *Rice*. Minneapolis: Lerner, 1985.
Latham, A. J. H. *Rice: The Primary Commodity*. London: Routledge, 1998.
Luh, Bor S. *Rice: Production and Utilization*. Westport, CT: AVI Publishing, 1980.
Rice: Chemistry and Technology. Bienvenido O. Juliano, ed. St. Paul, MN: American Society of Cereal Chemists, 1985.
Roberts, Jonathan. *The Origins of Fruits and Vegetables*. New York: Rizzoli, 2001.
Selsam, Millicent E. *The Plants We Eat*. New York: Morrow, 1981.
Van Nostrand's Scientific Encyclopedia, 8th ed., 2 vols. Douglas M. Considine and Glenn D. Considine, eds. New York: Van Nostrand Reinhold, 1995.
Vaughan, J. G., and C. A. Geissler. *The New Oxford Book of Plants*. New York: Oxford, 1997.

Index